Investigating water and rivers

Fred Martin

www.heinemann.co.uk/library

Visit our website to find out more information about **Heinemann Library** books.

To order:
☎ Phone 44 (0) 1865 888066
📄 Send a fax to 44 (0) 1865 314091
💻 Visit the Heinemann Bookshop at www.heinemann.co.uk/library to browse our catalogue and order online.

First published in Great Britain by Heinemann Library, Halley Court, Jordan Hill, Oxford OX2 8EJ, part of Harcourt Education. Heinemann is a registered trademark of Harcourt Education Ltd.

Editorial: Vicki Yates
Design: Dave Poole and Tokay Interactive Limited (www.tokay.co.uk)
Illustrations: Geoff Ward and International Mapping (www.internationalmapping.com)
Picture Research: Hannah Taylor
Production: Duncan Gilbert

Originated by Repro Multi Warna
Printed and bound in China by WKT Company Limited

10 digit ISBN: 0 431 03255 6   (Hardback)
13 digit ISBN: 978 0 431 03255 9 (Hardback)
10 09 08 07 06
10 9 8 7 6 5 4 3 2 1

10 digit ISBN: 0 431 03262 9   (Paperback)
13 digit ISBN: 978 0 431 03262 7 (Paperback)
10 09 08 07 06
10 9 8 7 6 5 4 3 2 1

British Library Cataloguing in Publication Data
Martin, Fred
Investigating water and rivers
910.9 ' 1693
A full catalogue record for this book is available from the British Library.

Acknowledgements
The publishers would like to thank the following for permission to reproduce photographs:
Corbis Royalty Free p. **10**; Corbis p. **21** (Roger Ressmeyer), p. **23** (NASA), p. **29** (Jim McDonald); p. **14** Digital Vision; Ecoscene p. **25** (John Millership); Empics p. **26** (PA/Toby Melville), p. **27** (Sarah Bruntlett); Geoscience Features Picture Library p. **16**; Getty Images pp. **4**, **9**, **11** (Photodisc), p. **7** (Ami Vitale), p. **20** (Stone), p. **22** (Taxi); Photodisc p. **8**; Robert Harding p. **28** (Nigel Francis); Science Photo Library p. **17** (Sally Bensusan (1987)); Skyscan p. **24** (I Bracegirdle); Still Pictures p. **13** (Jorgen Schytte); Topfoto.co.uk p. **12**; Topfoto p. **6** (The Image Works/Ellen Senisi).

Cover photograph of a waterfall and pool of water, reproduced with permission of Getty Images/The Image bank.

The publishers would like to thank Rebecca Harman, Rachel Bowles, Robyn Hardyman, and Caroline Landon for their assistance in the preparation of this book.

Every effort has been made to contact copyright holders of any material reproduced in this book. Any omissions will be rectified in subsequent printings if notice is given to the publishers.

All the Internet addresses (URLs) given in this book were valid at the time of going to press. However, due to the dynamic nature of the Internet, some addresses may have changed, or sites may have changed or ceased to exist since publication. While the author and Publishers regret any inconvenience this may cause readers, no responsibility for any such changes can be accepted by either the author or the Publishers.

Exploring further

Throughout this book you will find links to the Heinemann Explore CD-ROM and website at www.heinemannexplore.com. Follow the links to find out more about the topic.

Contents

Any words appearing in the text in bold, **like this**, are explained in the glossary.

Water everywhere

There is water all around you, in rivers and lakes, in the seas and oceans, in rocks under the ground, and even in the air.

Where can we find water locally?

You can find places where there is water in your area by looking at an Ordnance Survey map. Lakes and rivers are shown in blue. There may also be some **springs** where water comes out of the ground, and areas of bog or marsh where the ground is always wet.

There may be water in rocks under the ground. Some rocks, such as chalk, limestone, and sandstone, can hold water in cracks and small spaces between their grains. An underground store of water is called an **aquifer**.

Activity

Look at an Ordnance Survey map of your area and find all the evidence of water.

Look for:

- lakes and ponds
- rivers and streams
- springs and wells
- areas of bog or marsh.

■ *Nowhere in the UK is ever dry for very long. The Lake District in north-west England is one of the wettest places in the UK.*

Where can we find water in the world?

From space, the oceans and seas make the Earth look like a 'blue' planet. They cover about three-quarters of the Earth's surface. The deepest parts of the oceans are many miles deep.

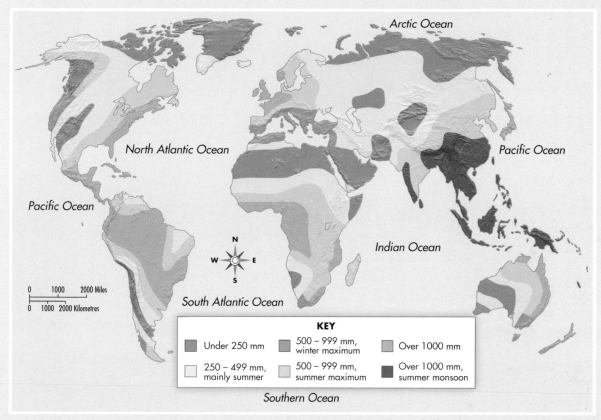

■ *This map shows the location of the world's oceans. It also shows how much rain falls around the world each year.*

On land, the amount of water varies from place to place. Some of the wettest places on Earth are in the hot areas near the **equator**. Here it can rain heavily every day, usually during a thunderstorm. Thunderstorms occur when the **climate** is **humid**.

There are other hot places that also get a lot of rain. In these areas the rain comes in seasons, rather than all year round. Can you think where these places might be?

Exploring further

On the Heinemann Explore website or CD-ROM go to Exploring > Our wet planet. Read the article 'Water all around' to find out which two gases make up water, and in what forms water can be found on Earth.

How does water get to where it is needed?

One problem with water is that there never seems to be the right amount of it in the right place at the right time.

Water at school

Water comes to and from your school in both natural and artificial ways. You can see signs of the natural ways by looking around the school buildings and grounds after it rains. Some rain falls on the grass and other surfaces that let the water sink in.

■ *On a hard surface, such as concrete, the water lies in puddles. Gradually the puddles dry up, as the Sun **evaporates** the water.*

Rain that falls on buildings flows into gutters then down drainpipes into the drains. You can make a map with arrows to show how rainwater comes to your school, and then flows away again.

Artificial ways of getting water include turning on a tap or flushing a toilet. This water comes from pipelines that carry fresh water to the school. Somewhere in the school grounds there is a **stopcock** that controls this flow of water.

Carrying water

You would not find it easy to carry all the water you use in a day, even for a short distance across the school grounds. However, in many of the world's countries, getting a daily water supply is difficult for lots of people.

Water for farming

Farmers need water for growing crops and rearing animals. Water can be brought to the fields in channels or pipes from rivers, **reservoirs**, or from underground. This is called **irrigation**.

People have been irrigating their fields for thousands of years. In Egypt, farmers use equipment, such as the **shaduf,** to bring water up from the River Nile. This water then flows over the fields, helping the crops to grow. A modern way to irrigate the land is to use pipelines and water sprinklers.

■ *These girls from Malawi in Africa have to walk to a well or river to fetch their water, then carry it back to their homes. This can take several hours, every day. Even then, the water is often not safe to drink because it is not clean.*

Using water

Who uses water and what do they use it for?

Everyone uses water. Think about the many different ways that you use water during a typical day. You use it for drinking, cooking, washing, and flushing a toilet. People in other countries have the same needs for water. In some countries, people cannot easily get to a supply of water that is safe to use. This makes their daily life difficult.

Water for work and play

Some uses of water might not be very obvious to us. In the UK, water is used in **power stations** to generate electricity. Water is also used in factories, for example for making paper, cooling machinery, washing fibres, and cleaning containers.

Farmers need water for growing crops and rearing animals. If they do not have enough water they cannot produce enough food for everyone in the country. In countries that do not have enough money to buy food from other countries, this often leads to **famine** and starvation.

■ *We are lucky to have enough water to use it for leisure activities, like swimming.*

Activity

1 List all the ways in which you use water at school.

2 Imagine you have to use less water. Choose the uses on your list that you could do without, and the uses where you could use less water.

Water consumption

People in the world's richest countries use far more water than people in poorer countries. Some of these uses are not really necessary. You can waste 20 litres of water each day just by leaving the tap running while you clean your teeth. People in poorer countries, who have to walk a long way to fetch their water, are not likely to waste it, and will use less of it.

The effects of wasting water

Wasting water can cause problems. If there is a long dry period in the summer, the **reservoirs** will start to run out of water. Our supply may then be rationed. A drastic action is to shut off the supply and make people collect their water from special taps in the street or from water tankers. Another solution to water shortages is to build more reservoirs. These can store more water from the wet months, so there will be enough to get through the dry months.

■ *A simple way to reduce the amount of water that is wasted is to ban the use of hosepipes and sprinklers during a dry summer.*

Is all water usable?

Not all water is safe for us to use. We cannot drink salt water from the sea. Drinking water that is **polluted** or that has germs living in it is not safe either. Many diseases are caused by unclean water.

- *Even though there is a huge amount of water in the sea, we cannot drink it because it has salt in it. People cannot drink salt water because it makes them ill.*

Water and disease

In the UK during the 19th century, many people in the large industrial cities died from a disease called cholera. Eventually people realized that this disease was caused by people drinking polluted water. After this discovery, the water in the UK was cleaned up and became safer to drink.

Unsafe water in the world today

There are still many countries where the water supply is not safe to drink. More than 40 per cent of the world's population is affected in this way. In the poorest countries, about ten people die every minute from diseases linked to dirty water. A safe and clean supply of water would be one of the best ways to save lives in these places.

How can water be made usable?

Water can be made safe by some simple methods. Boiling water kills the germs in it. Tablets can also be used to clean water. Larger pieces of pollution can be removed from water by **filtering** it. In Britain, water in **reservoirs** is kept clean by making sure that pollution cannot get into it.

Water that has been used is taken through huge underground pipes called sewers, to **sewage** treatment works. Here dirty water is filtered through layers of gravel until it is clean again and can be reused.

Sea water has salt in it so people can't drink it. Salt water can be made safe to drink by taking the salt out of it. It is expensive to do this, but in hot, dry countries it is one of the only ways to produce enough water for everyone.

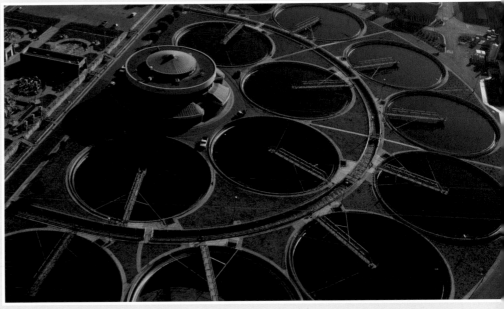

■ *Dirty water is cleaned and made safe to use again in sewage treatment works.*

See for yourself

1 Find pictures on the Internet of a sewage treatment works.
2 Write a paragraph about what goes on there.
3 Visit a sewage treatment works if there is one near your school.

Exploring further

On the Heinemann Explore website or CD-ROM go to Exploring > Our wet planet. Read the article 'Safe water' to find out about water-borne diseases and where they are most common.

Who owns water and who pays for it?

You do not have to pay anyone for the rain, but you do have to pay for the water that comes into your home. Water companies supply water. They are businesses, just like any other industry.

The water business in the UK

The areas of the UK are supplied with water by local water companies. Water companies build and look after the **reservoirs** that store water. They might also take water directly from rivers or from beneath the ground. They do this by drilling **boreholes** to get water that has sunk into the rocks underground.

■ *Cheddar reservoir in Somerset, UK.*

Water companies manage **sewage** treatment works that clean the water so it can be reused. Water is taken to homes, buildings, and factories through underground pipelines. Water companies must look after these pipelines.

For most people in the UK, the amount they pay for their water depends on the value of their home. It it not affected by how much water they use. Other people install a water meter in their homes, to measure how much water they use. They only pay for the amount they use.

Activity

Do you know how the water you use is paid for? Find out by asking one of the grown ups you live with. Would you use more or less water if you paid for it through a meter?

Water Aid

One of the main ways to help people in poorer countries to have a better standard of living is to improve their water supply. This will make them healthier and help them to farm more successfully. It will also save them a lot of time and effort in walking to collect water.

Many UK water companies are trying to help bring clean water to people in countries where the water supply is unsafe. They raise money from their customers in the UK. The money they raise goes towards a project called Water Aid.

In one district in Tanzania in Africa, water pumps were paid for with money from Water Aid. The pumps were installed by local people. Before they had pumps, the villagers had to walk 8 km (5 miles) to the nearest water. They had to queue for hours to fill their jars. Now, with the pumps, they can wash properly in clean water and have safe water to drink. There is much less illness in the district.

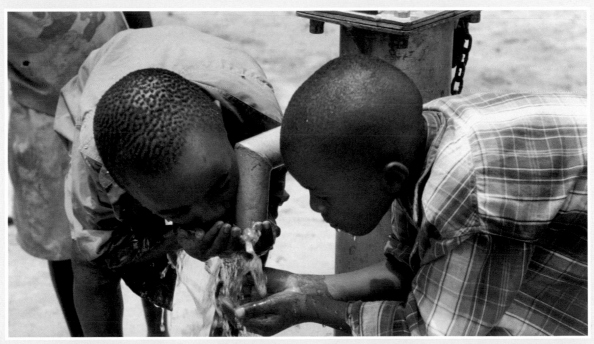

■ *Money raised by people in the UK helps people in poor countries to have access to safe water.*

The water cycle

Where does water come from?

There is water on the ground, under the ground, in the sea, and in the air. Water is found in different forms, some that you can see and some that you cannot see. Water is one of the main reasons why there is life on our planet.

Forms of water

Water is made of two gases called oxygen and hydrogen. You can see water when it is a liquid in the sea, lakes, and rivers. You can also see it when it is a solid, as ice.

Water in the air exists as a gas called **water vapour**. You cannot see water vapour, but you can tell it is there when the **weather** is hot and feels sticky. This is called **humid** weather.

Water changes between water vapour, liquid, and ice. This mostly depends on the **temperature**. When water is heated, it changes to a gas. When it cools down, it changes back to liquid water. When it is freezing, liquid water becomes ice.

Moving water

Most of the water on Earth is in the seas and oceans. The Sun heats the water and changes it into water vapour in the air. This is called **evaporation**. When the water vapour becomes colder, it changes into tiny water droplets. This is called **condensation**. When lots of droplets form together, we see them as clouds.

■ *When air containing water vapour is cooled, the water condenses to form clouds.*

Rain falls back to the ground from the clouds. It sinks into the ground or runs off over the ground. The rainwater then finds its way into rivers. The rivers take the water back to the sea. The way in which water moves from the ground and sea into the air, then back to the land as rain, is called the **water cycle**.

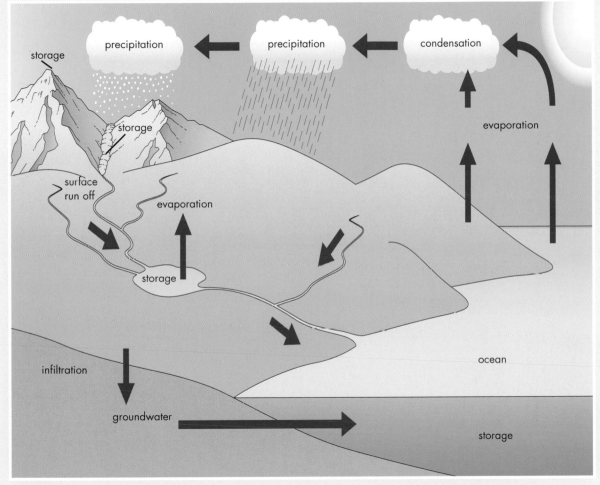

- *These are the processes involved in the water cycle. Water is constantly moving around the surface of the Earth.*

Exploring further

On the Heinemann Explore website or CD-ROM go to Resources > Our wet planet. Watch the animation on the water cycle to make sure you understand each stage in the process.

Where does water go to?

There are plenty of clues around you about where water goes to. You can even see it in your own school grounds. Watch where the rainwater goes after a shower and you will see what happens on a small scale.

Flowing water

In the landscape beyond the school, some rain **evaporates** straight back into the air. Some is taken up through the roots of trees and into their leaves, before it goes back into the air. Water also sinks into the ground to form **groundwater**. It can appear on the surface again as a **spring**.

■ *Underground water can appear on the surface as a spring.*

Water falling on slopes can flow off the surface as **run-off**. It soon starts to flow in narrow channels called **rills**. The rills flow into each other to make streams, and these join together to make wider and deeper streams. In mountain areas, the **headwaters** of a river can be made from thousands of tiny rills and streams.

Streams join each other to become **tributary** rivers. A tributary is a river that joins a larger river. The more tributary rivers there are, the more water flows into the main river. Where two rivers meet is called a **confluence**.

Soon there is a whole **network** of streams and rivers. All the rills, streams, and rivers that flow into each other make a network called a **river system**.

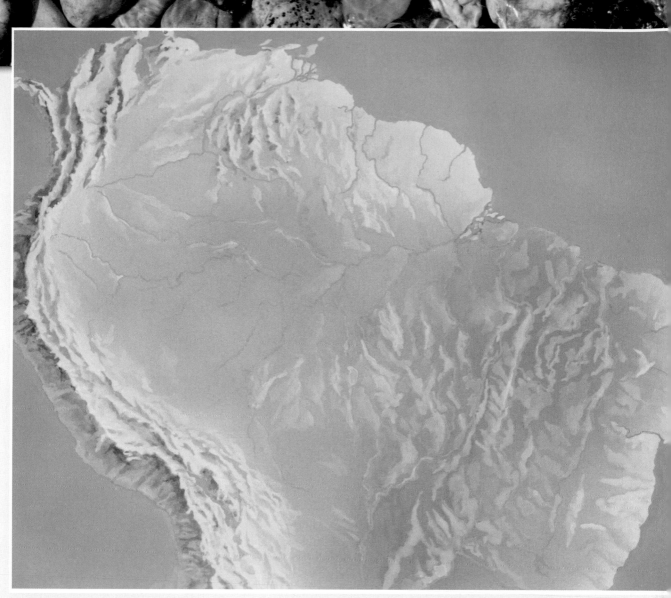

■ *This illustration of the Amazon River and its tributaries shows how the network of streams and rivers forms a pattern that looks like the veins on a leaf.*

A drainage basin

The rills, streams, and rivers that flow over the surface of the land are the natural drains for rainwater. They take it away to the sea. This is why the streams and rivers of an area are called the area's **drainage**.

The whole area drained by a river system is called a **drainage basin**. The sides of a drainage basin are the slopes and ridges that run round the highest points around its edge. Rain that falls on one side of a ridge flows into one drainage basin. Rain on the other side falls into a different drainage basin.

The line that divides one drainage basin from another is called a **watershed**. Water flows out of the drainage basin. Rivers transport water through a **valley** and take it away to the sea.

Where does the river go to?

The route that a river follows is called its **course**. Most rivers start in the mountains. The place where a river starts is called its **source**. Here the river is narrow and it flows fast. This area is called the upper course. The river flows down the mountain and on to flatter land. This area is called the middle course and here the river widens.

As the river approaches the sea, it enters the area called the lower course. Here it widens even more and appears to slow down. However, the water here has tremendous power to sweep away everything it carries – including people! Finally the river flows into the sea, at the place called its **mouth**.

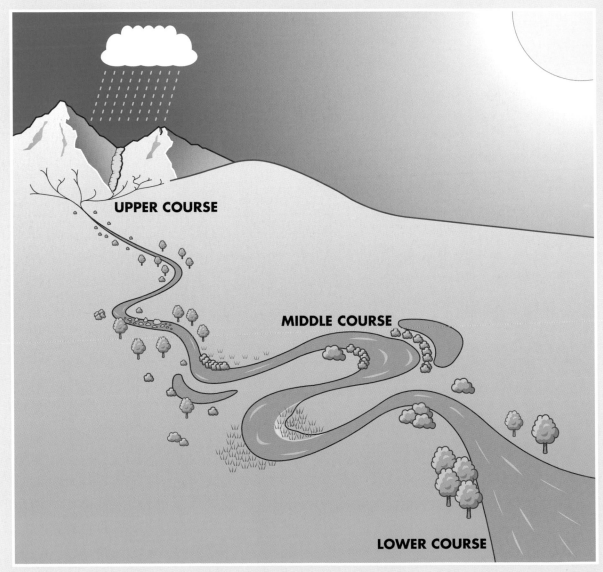

UPPER COURSE

MIDDLE COURSE

LOWER COURSE

■ *The course of a river.*

Activity

1 Look at an Ordnance Survey map of your area and find the nearest river (hint: it will be blue).

2 Can you find the river's source (it might be beyond the edge of the map)?

3 Follow the route of the river.

4 Find the names of other rivers that flow into it.

5 Your river may flow into an even bigger river as a tributary. Follow its course until it reaches the sea.

The source of the River Trent

The River Trent flows through the centre of England. It is 274 km (170 miles) long, and is the second longest river in England. It rises about 20 km (12 miles) to the north-east of Stoke-on-Trent, in the hills of north Staffordshire. Several streams flow from the hills and join together to make the Trent even bigger. These are called **tributaries**.

The River Trent's route to the sea

The Trent takes a long, curving route to the sea. It flows south towards Stafford, but before it reaches Stafford it heads east towards Derby and Nottingham. After Nottingham it changes direction again, heading north. It flows out to the sea in the Humber **estuary** near Hull in Yorkshire.

Several larger tributary rivers join the Trent along its course. The Rivers Tame and Dove flow into it near Burton-on-Trent. The River Derwent, which flows through Derby, and the River Soar, from Leicester, then join it. Just before the Trent enters the Humber estuary, the River Ouse flows in from the east.

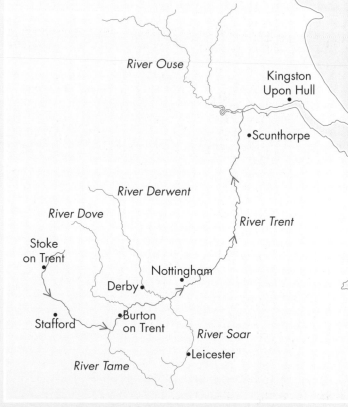

■ *This map shows the route of the River Trent.*

How do rivers change the landscape?

Rivers change the shape of the land as they flow over it. As a river flows along its **course** it carves out a channel. This happens over thousands or even millions of years. This is how **valleys** are formed.

Eroding the land

Soil and rock are worn away as the river flows over them, carving out a channel. This process is called **erosion**. The rock and soil are carried along by the river and are called its **load**. Erosion is changing the shape and depth of the river's channel all the time.

■ *A fast-flowing river may look cloudy, as it can carry a big load. This river and its load will cause much erosion to the landscape.*

River valleys

Rivers flow through valleys. This is because most valleys are cut out of the land by the rivers that flow through them. Valleys in mountain areas are often deep with steep sides. They are V-shaped, with almost no flat land at the bottom. There is just enough space in the bottom of the valley for the river to flow through it.

■ *In their upper courses, rivers carve V-shaped valleys into the landscape.*

A deep valley with steep sides is called a **gorge** or **canyon**. At the Avon Gorge near Bristol the River Avon has cut a deep and steep-sided valley through the hills. In mountain areas in Britain, the biggest valleys are deep and U-shaped, with steep sides. **Glaciers** of ice carved out these valleys. The ice melted a long time ago and rivers now flow through them.

A valley in the lower course of a river is usually wider, with gently sloping sides. The valley bottom is called the **flood plain**. It is usually wide and flat. It forms when a river bursts it banks and floods the valley floor. When this happens the river drops its load. This is called **deposition**. Flood plains are **fertile** and are often used for farming. In the USA, the floodplain of the Mississippi River is over 100 km (about 62 miles) wide.

Around the bend

Rivers almost never flow in a straight line. They wind and bend across their **valley** bottoms. A river bend is called a **meander**.

■ *A river with a winding course is said to be meandering.*

The mouth of the river

The place where a river joins the sea is its **mouth**. At the mouth, a river **deposits** its load to form a **delta**. This is a muddy pile of sediment that looks like a giant fan from the air.

■ *At the mouth of the River Nile in Egypt, deposits have built up to form a delta where the river enters the Mediterranean Sea.*

Exploring further

Go to the Heinemann Explore website or CD-ROM and click on Resources. Find the videos showing the formation of a canyon and a waterfall. Think about how each feature is formed.

Case study: the River Trent

The River Trent is like other rivers in many ways. It changes the landscape it flows through by **eroding**, transporting, and **depositing** rock and soil.

Landforms in the River Trent valley

In the river's middle **course**, you can see from the colour of the water that it is wearing away the land. It is brown and murky, especially after a long period of rain. Tiny grains of soil that make the river water brown have eroded from the land.

By the time the river reaches Burton-on-Trent it is wider and deeper. Its valley is also much wider, and the sides slope more gently.

■ *The River Trent does not flow in a straight line through its valley. Its **meanders** help to wear away the valley sides to make it wider and produce a flat flood plain.*

Land use in the River Trent valley

The River Trent also affects the **human features** of the land it flows through. Most of the land in the valley is used for farming, especially for rearing cattle, but there can be a problem with flooding on the **flood plain**. Towns and cities have grown up alongside the river, such as Burton-on-Trent, Nottingham, and Newark. Bridges were built at these places. This helped them to become bases for trade and industry.

■ *The River Trent is useful for many things. Here you can see that a power station has been built on its banks. People also use the river for leisure activities like sailing.*

The Trent valley is also used for **power stations**. These are beside the river, and use the water to generate electricity and for cooling the machinery. Railway lines along the flat valley bottom bring coal to the power stations.

In many places along the river there are small ponds and lakes. These are sand and gravel pits. The sand and gravel were deposited there by the river over thousands of years. They are dug out and then used mainly for building. Some of the pits are still in use, but many have closed down. Some have been made into **nature reserves**. One area of old gravel pits at Holme Pierrepont, near Nottingham, has become Britain's biggest centre for water sports.

The dangers of flooding

All rivers flood at some time. It is a natural thing for them to do. Therefore, people who live along the banks of a river run the risk of being flooded from time to time.

Flood time

A river floods when its channel is not big enough to carry all the water that flows into it. When this happens, the river either breaks through its banks or flows over the top of them.

In the UK, flooding is usually caused by several weeks of heavy rain or by melting snow. The ground becomes **waterlogged**. This means that it cannot hold any more water. Instead, rainwater flows off the land as **run-off**, into the rivers. This extra water causes the river to flood.

Flood defences

To prevent floods, more water needs to be kept in the river channel. One way to do this is to make the river banks higher with **levees**. These are narrow ridges along the tops of the banks. Another way is to remove mud and stones from the river, so there is more space for the extra floodwater. Planting trees can also stop too much water getting into a river in a short time.

■ *When a river breaks its banks it causes huge problems for everyone in the area.*

The River Trent floods

The River Trent flows through a broad **valley** with a flat bottom for much of its **course**. This makes it likely to flood. There is not much anyone can do to stop the water flooding their homes.

There were severe floods along the River Trent in 1947. After this, flood defences were built in some places to stop it happening again. However, not everywhere was protected, and in November 2000 parts of Burton-on-Trent were flooded.

■ *This flooding was caused by the River Trent in November 2000.*

Activity

Imagine you are a journalist. Write a newspaper report about the effects of flooding on the people who live near a river. Think about the these points:

- Who has been affected by the flood?
- How have people tried to protect their property?
- How do people feel about the damage the flood has caused?
- What could people do to prevent flooding in the future?

Exploring further

Go to the Heinemann Explore website or CD-ROM, click on Exploring > Rivers at work. Read the article 'Living with floods' and make a list of all the causes of floods.

Using rivers

Rivers affect people's lives in many different ways. This influences how they think and feel about them.

See for yourself

1 Visit a river near your school or home with an adult. Make a sketch of the river and its surroundings.
2 Label all the features present, such as: a V-shaped **valley**, boulders, waterfalls, **meanders**, a floodplain, trees, picnic sites, houses, factories, and roads.
3 Write a paragraph describing the river and how you feel about it. If you use the river for leisure, you may like it. If your house has been flooded by the river, it may make you angry.

Enjoying rivers

Many people use rivers for leisure. It is pleasant to go for a picnic next to a river, or to walk alongside one. Some rivers have spectacular scenery, such as **canyons** and waterfalls. Some rivers are popular places for taking a holiday. There are holiday cruises through Egypt along the River Nile and along the River Rhine in Germany.

▪ *People enjoy visiting Swallow Falls, in Betws-y-Coed, North Wales, as it has dramatic scenery.*

Fishing and farming

In some countries, fish from rivers are an important part of people's diets. It is therefore important to keep rivers clean so that fish can live in them. **Irrigation** water for farming can be obtained from rivers, through pipes or channels.

River transport

In the past, it was easier to move goods on rivers than on roads. A river that can be used by boats is called a navigable river. A navigable river has to be deep, wide, and not too fast flowing, so the boats can use it safely.

■ *Large rivers, such as the Rhine in Germany, are still used to transport goods, like cars.*

Power from rivers

River water can be used in **power stations**, to generate electricity and to cool the machinery. This is why power stations are often built next to rivers, such as the River Trent and River Severn in the UK.

Activity

Make a list of all the ways you can use a river. Include ways in which rivers are used today and ways in which they were used in the past. Use the Internet and reference books to find out the names of rivers that are used or were used in these ways.

Glossary

aquifer underground store of water

borehole well drilled into rocks to get water that has sunk into the rocks underground

climate the average weather conditions over a long period of time

condensation the change from water vapour to liquid water droplets

confluence place where two rivers meet

course route that a river follows

delta muddy pile of sediment formed when a river meets the sea. It looks like a giant fan from the air.

deposition when a river drops its load

drainage the streams and rivers of an area

drainage basin area drained by a river system

equator imaginary line around the middle of the Earth

erosion wearing away of rocks and soil by wind, water, or ice

estuary place where a river widens out as it enters the sea

evaporation when liquid water changes into water vapour

famine when there is not enough food for people to eat

fertile full of nutrients and so able to support the growing of crops

filtering passing water through filters, such as gravel, to clean it

flood plain flat valley bottom

glacier slow-moving river of ice

gorge/canyon valley that is very deep with sides that are almost vertical

groundwater water that has sunk underground

headwaters streams from the sources of a river

human features all the things in a place made by humans, such as housing, factories, and roads

humid hot and wet

irrigate to supply a place or area with water, for example to grow crops

levee narrow ridge along the top of a river bank

load rock and soil carried along by the river

meander bend in a river

mouth end of a river where it flows into the sea

nature reserve area of land where the wildlife is protected

network group of connected streams and rivers

polluted dirty

power station factory that generates electricity

reservoir lake made by humans for storing water

rill small channel of water

river system all the rills, streams, and rivers that flow into each other

run-off water running over the land surface

sewage liquid and solid waste from people

shaduf simple machine using a bucket and poles to lift water from a river

source place where a river starts

spring place where water comes out of the ground

stopcock tap that controls the flow of water into a building

temperature how hot or cold something is

tributary smaller river that joins a main river

valley landform created by a river eroding the landscape

Water Aid charity that aims to provide clean water for people in less economically developed countries

water cycle the way that water moves from the ground and sea into the air, then back to the land as rain

water vapour water as a gas

waterlogged when no more rainwater can soak into the ground

watershed line that divides one drainage basin from another

weather the condition of the atmosphere at one point in time, which can change every day

Find out more

Books

Mapping the UK: Mapping lives, Louise Spilsbury (Heinemann Library, 2005)

Awesome Forces of Nature: Raging Floods, Louise and Richard Spilsbury (Heinemann Library, 2003)

Rivers through Time, Rob Bowden (Heinemann Library, 2005)

Landscapes and People, Earth's changing rivers, Neil Morris (Raintree, 2004)

Websites

www.environment-agency.co.uk/fun
The environment agency has information about water and rivers in the UK and fact sheets and advice about flooding.

www.sln.org.uk/trentweb
Join Fergal the Frog for a trip down the River Trent to see lots of aerial photos of the river area, and some maps too.

www.heinemannexplore.com
Check out the water section of the Explore geography site to find out even more about water and rivers.

Index